General court Massachusetts

Proceedings of the Massachusetts Senate on the occasion of

the reception of the portrait of General David Cobb

1801-1805

General court Massachusetts

Proceedings of the Massachusetts Senate on the occasion of the reception of the portrait of General David Cobb
1801-1805

ISBN/EAN: 9783337173913

Printed in Europe, USA, Canada, Australia, Japan

Cover: Foto ©ninafisch / pixelio.de

More available books at **www.hansebooks.com**

PROCEEDINGS

OF THE

MASSACHUSETTS SENATE

On the Occasion of the Reception

OF THE

PORTRAIT OF GENERAL DAVID COBB,

President of that Body, 1801–1805.

FEBRUARY 23, 1882.

———•◦•———

CAMBRIDGE:
JOHN WILSON AND SON.
University Press.
1882.

THE account which is given in the following pages of the Proceedings in the Massachusetts Senate on the 23d ultimo, is offered by the undersigned as a token of his respect and veneration for the memory of the distinguished man whose career and public services are eloquently portrayed in the addresses made on that occasion.

Samuel C. Cobb.

BOSTON, *March, 1882.*

Thursday, Feb. 23, 1882, was assigned for the public exercises, connected with the reception by the Senate of the portrait of GEN. DAVID COBB, the gift of his grandson Hon. Samuel C. Cobb. The occasion was one of remarkable interest, and was graced by the attendance of a distinguished company of ladies and gentlemen. There were present among others Hon. Robert C. Winthrop, Hon. Marshall P. Wilder, Hon. Samuel A. Green, Mayor of Boston, Rev. Samuel K. Lothrop, D.D., Dr. Henry I. Bowditch, Dr. Charles D. Homans, Hon. Samuel L. Crocker, Hon. E. H. Bennett, Hon. Ellis Ames, Hon. Uriel Crocker, Curtis Guild, Esq., Justin Winsor, Esq., Abbott Lawrence, Esq. The exercises formed a fitting commemoration both of the subject of the portrait and of the birthday of Washington,[1] whose friendship and companionship in arms he shared.

[1] February 22 was a holiday, on which the Senate was not in session.

PROCEEDINGS.

THE Senate being called to order at two o'clock, prayer was offered by the Chaplain, Rev. EDMUND DOWSE, as follows : —

ALMIGHTY GOD, thou hast ordained that those who pass away from the earth, and are no longer personally present, may exert a salutary influence in forming the character and life of those who come after them. We feel that they are speaking to us in silent but powerful language, — by their good works while living, by their historical records, and by their life-like forms, that look down upon us from the walls of our private dwellings and public halls. We thank thee for these works of art, and we pray that they may not only prove sources of rich pleasure, but incentives to fidelity in duty, and to the practice of all that was pure, noble, and praiseworthy in the character and lives of those whom they represent. And we pray thee to direct and prosper this Senate in the duties and privileges of this day, and thine shall be the praise forever,

AMEN.

On motion of Hon. ANDREW C. STONE, Senator from Essex, the reading of the Journal was dispensed with.

The PRESIDENT OF THE SENATE read the following communication : —

BOSTON, 15th February, 1882.

The Hon. ROBERT R. BISHOP, *President of the Senate :* —

DEAR SIR, — Understanding from you that there is a desire to procure for the Senate Chamber portraits of past presidents of that body, I have taken the liberty of sending to the State House, directed to your care, a portrait of General DAVID COBB, which I respectfully ask may be added to the gallery belonging to the Commonwealth.

The original portrait was painted by Gilbert Stuart in 1809 or 1810, and the copy which I send you is by Edgar Parker of this city. It gives me, as the only direct male descendant of General COBB, of the name, now living, much pleasure to present his portrait to the State, and have it placed in a position where it will perpetuate the memory of this distinguished son of Massachusetts.

The name of DAVID COBB occupies a high place on the roll of honor of our State, and his services will always be held in grateful remembrance. The story of his eventful life is one of interest and importance, covering, as it does, the most momentous period in the history of this government immediately following the Declaration of Independence. He witnessed the events which preceded the revolutionary struggle, having been born in the middle of the last century, and, after a service of seven years as an officer of the Continental Army, he saw the political independence of this nation firmly established. In 1784 he returned to his native State, where he became prominent in public affairs, and filled for more than thirty years positions of honor and trust with marked ability and fidelity.

May his portrait speak to us, and to coming generations, of the noble virtues and patriotic ardor which inspired our fathers to carry forward to a successful termination the great struggle which made us a free and independent people.

I am, Mr. President, your obedient servant,

SAMUEL C. COBB.

The PRESIDENT then addressed the Senate as follows : —

In presenting this letter from a distinguished citizen of Massachusetts, and the valuable gift which accompanies it, the Senate would hardly pardon me, I am sure, if I did not give some expression to its sense, both of the fitness and grace of the act, and also of the grand character of the man whose portrait, by the act, is to speak to us from these walls. That character is interwoven in our history, and is a part of the texture and fibre of our institutions. By him, and such as he, the institutions and structure of the Commonwealth and of the country were moulded and fashioned at the critical period of the formation of the state and the nation as independent governments. He was no inconspicuous actor in that work. Trained as a young man amid the events which led up to the Revolution, when that event occurred he abandoned like Warren the practice of a physician, which he was just beginning, and threw himself with ardor and inspiration into the struggle ; and, from that time to nearly the close of a long life, he bore a conspicuous part in some form of the public service. Appointed by Washington a member of his staff, and continuing a member of his military family during the war ; appointed by Hancock at its close to be a Judge of the Court of Common Pleas, and elected almost simultaneously by the Legislature as Major-General of the Massachusetts Militia ; afterwards, a member of the

House of Representatives of the State for four years, and its Speaker; a member of Congress; member of the State Senate, and its President for four years; and Lieutenant-Governor, — these offices attest the trust reposed in him by his Commander-in-chief and by his fellow-citizens.

The grateful duty of speaking in detail of the events of his life properly falls to, and will be fitly performed by, another, the Senator who represents the district which was the home of General Cobb for the most of his life, the principal town of which sent him, as a colleague of Robert Treat Paine, as a representative to the first General Court ever held in Massachusetts independently of royal authority, and in which, twice in the same year, he subdued a mob-gathered to stop the holding of the courts of justice, and uttered the memorable declaration, so clearly displaying his character, " For this day I will sit as a judge or die as a general." But the magnificent lesson of his life, the enthusiasm of his spirit, and his work in our institutions, appeal to us all. A grand old hero, — type for all years and generations, of honor, of patriotism, and of chivalry !

As by this act, alike of filial and of patriotic duty, performed by his grandson, inheriting and in the exercise of the same spirit, this portrait takes its place in the Senate gallery, what a grand company it enters; what a company of kindred spirits of the earlier and the later time ! Winthrop is here, and has been here for generations, to speak from these walls. It is the same picture, it is believed, which hung in the mansion-house of Governor Winthrop on Milk Street, and of which the story is related that, after his death, an old Indian Sagamore, visiting the room where it hung, ran out in great excitement, crying, " He is alive, he is alive, he is alive !"   It is the same portrait, no doubt, which John Adams says, with the portraits of Endicott and Bradstreet, also here, and with that of Belcher, not here, hung in obscure corners of the old Council Chamber at the time when Sam Adams appeared before Governor Hutchinson and demanded the withdrawal of the troops from Boston.   Of the early history of the portrait of Endicott little is known beyond this reference.   Here, also, is Leverett, appearing, not in the military dress of his younger life, but with shaven face, his beard as is said having been laid aside at the court of the Protector, and with the white flowing locks of old age.   Here, also, is the glowing face of Bradstreet, and the portrait of Bernet.   Here are the majestic features of Governor Sumner, painted in 1792, the subject clad in the robes of a Justice of the Supreme Judicial Court of this State, which office he then held, the portrait presented to the Commonwealth by his son, General Sumner, and received in 1862.   Here, also, are the portraits of Governor Eustis, presented to the Senate by " A Republican Institution " in 1874, and of Robert Rantoul, Jr., placed in the Senate Chamber in 1859.   Here, also, are the trophies sent by Stark from Bennington, and, more precious even than they, the king's arm, captured by Captain John Parker on the morning of the 19th of April, 1775, — the first firearm taken in the War of the Revolution, — and the musket carried by Captain Parker himself on that day.   You do not need to be reminded whose words they are which I repeat : " Dear shades of all our fathers, whose hearts were fired by an ardor which no taunts, no threats, no powers could ever discourage or cause to falter, be present now, be present always; in every hour of your country's danger, in every moment when hearts grow faint or knees grow weak. Be thou immortal hanging on the Senate walls! . . . And, oh, if in any degenerate hour Massachusetts should falter or quail, may some weird hand beat the old drum which hangs beneath the roof-tree of the Senate, give aim to the arm which spoke for liberty on the morning of the 19th of April, 1775, and may it march before the conquering hosts of re-enkindled patriotism and re-invigorated devotion!" Whose words were they or could they be but those of John A. Andrew, and on what occasion of public apprehension could they have been spoken but in January, 1861, three months before the firing on Fort Sumter, when the fate and the future of his country were trembling in suspense!

The full account given by John Adams of the portraits in the Council Chamber, from which I have quoted, is as follows: "Two portraits, at more than full length, of King Charles the Second, and of King James the Second, in splendid golden frames, were hung up on the most conspicuous sides of the apartment. If my young eyes or old memory have not deceived me, these were as fine pictures as I ever saw; the colors of the royal ermines, and long, flowing robes, were the most glowing, the figures the most noble and graceful, the features the most distinct and characteristic, far superior to those of the King and Queen of France, in the Senate Chamber of Congress, — these were worthy of the pencils of Rubens and Vandyke. There was no painter in England capable of them at the time. They had been sent over, without frames, in Governor Pownall's time, but he was no admirer of Charles or James. The pictures were stowed away in a garret among rubbish till Governor Bernard came, who had them cleaned, superbly framed, and placed in council for the admiration and imitation of all men, — no doubt with the advice and concurrence of Hutchinson and all his nebula of stars and satellites." To these, he says, " might be added, and should be added, little miserable likenesses of Governor Winthrop, Governor Bradstreet, Governor Endicott, and Governor Belcher, hung up in obscure corners of the room." [1]

We have no desire, certainly, for the restoration of the splendors of the provincial Council Chamber, nor any regrets at the disappearance of the portraits of the kings. The stones which these builders rejected, the worthies of the colonial period, have indeed become the chief corner-stones of our temple, and are exalted to our highest places of honor. To these we have added the heroes and great men of the Revolution, and of later times. Welcome to this congenial company a noble and congenial spirit!

I have to thank heartily on behalf of the Senate the distinguished gentlemen who have honored the occasion of the presentation of this portrait with their presence. Some of them, I am sure, are gentlemen who knew the subject of the portrait. The distinguished and honored descendant and representative of the first Governor of Massachusetts; the oldest living President of the Senate, holding that office in 1842 and 1844; the distinguished and venerable President of the Senate in 1850; the physician, a remarkable coincidence, who attended General

[1] John Adams's Works, vol. 10, pp. 245, 249.

Cobb in his last sickness, as I am just informed; the presence of these and many others is especially gratifying at such a commemoration.

I await such action as the Senate may deem proper.

Hon. GEORGE G. CROCKER, Senator from Suffolk, then offered the following resolution : —

Resolved, That we accept from the Hon. Samuel C. Cobb the portrait of David Cobb, President of this body from the year 1801 to the year 1805, to be hung in honorable position within this Senate Chamber; with our thanks for the gift, we also desire to express to the generous grandson our strong appreciation and approval of the dutiful and praiseworthy motives which have led him thus to show the esteem and veneration in which he justly holds the memory of his illustrious grandsire. Great as are the merits and intrinsic value of the painting, we feel that they dwindle into insignificance when compared with the wealth of inspiration and impulse which we and our successors may gather from the study of the noble life which the portrait commemorates. David Cobb, physician, warrior, judge, and statesman, we welcome your presence here, that those who enter this hall may be moved to emulate the lofty and patriotic purpose which ruled your life.

Hon. WILLIAM REED, Jr., Senator from Bristol, said : —

The brave soldier, devoted patriot, wise physician, and discreet jurist, whose likeness the painter's hand has laid on yonder canvas, was, as you have remarked, Mr. President, for many years the most distinguished citizen of that district in which I now live, where he was born, and where his ashes lie. The shaven face, quaintly cut coat, and lace ruffles, tell the story of the gliding days between that time and this better than I can number them, and carry us back to that period in the political life of our Commonwealth, when, just emerging from the struggle with the mother country, the new nation of the west had girt up its loins to perpetuate its individual existence, and fortify that liberty which had been won by such a generous expenditure of blood and treasure, — nay, to a period far anterior to this, for the span of his years was fourscore and two. It brought him up within the live period of, perhaps, one third of the members of this present Senate, two of whom, at least, had almost reached man's estate when he passed away, and one of whom — the honorable Senator from the Cape district at my right — remembers him as he was in the flesh. It bore him back, also, to that distant colonial time, which to us at this later day seems almost as nebulous as the Homeric period.

General David Cobb was born in Attleborough, Bristol County, on the 14th of September, 1748. King William's war, Queen Anne's war, King George's war, were over, but the lilies of France and the red cross of St. George had not been furled and laid away in inglorious peace, the sport of moth and rust, but fluttered still in threatening rivalry from Maine to the Gulf. The brief peace which preceded the final tournament was only a troubled calm in which the combatants lay upon their arms for a breathing spell, and listened with alert ears for the bugle blast and war whoop. Washington was then a young surveyor in the Virginian wilderness; Franklin, in the prime of life, had just begun to investigate the pranks of the forked lightning in the Philadelphia skies; and all the great leaders of public opinion at home, and ragged continentals on the bloody fields of the yet unborn Revolution, were in the first flush of manhood, and gaining, in these stirring times of strife between two giant European powers for the boundless

forests and broad savannas of the new world, that experience which was to steel their hearts and nerve their
arms for the still more bitter struggle scarcely a generation later. Even Braddock had not yet crossed the sea
to find his fate in the Pennsylvania wilderness. Born
when the air was full of martial sounds, and hearing
daily of the tented field, the lonely watch, the bivouac,
and the camp fire, it was perfectly natural that in later
days the country boy should turn away from the busy
avocations of peace to follow the drum. He was seven
years old when Braddock's fated campaign sent a thrill
of horror slowly creeping through the colonies. He
was eleven when Wolfe and Montcalm lay on the field
of battle before Quebec; he was fifteen when France
assented to that peace which stripped her of all her
American possessions save a few beggarly fishing stations near Newfoundland, and left only scattered Cana-
dian *voyageurs* to sing in their liquid tongue of the long
years of chivalric enterprise and daring wasted in thread-
ing the giant wildernesses and skimming the great lakes
for the benefit of a more fortunate antagonistic race.

Scholarly in all his instincts, the lad's thoughts natu-
rally tended to the University at Cambridge, even then
beginning upon the second century of its existence, and,
after a few years spent in study in the town of Braintree,
in 1762 he was matriculated at Harvard, and in 1766
emerged from academic restraints and began the study
of medicine in Boston. He was then eighteen years old
and full of that spirit which, even at that time, had made
Boston the hot-bed of resistance to British aggression,
and a seething political caldron. Indeed, the spirit of
resistance was ingrained into New England nature by

the character of the transatlantic experiment, and the climatic surroundings. It is the spirit of resistance which makes men men, and to its proper direction and cultivation all national and personal success is due. Not that stolid reliance on fate which filled the trenches of Plevna with Moslem slain, for stolidly fighting for a cause about which one knows nothing and dying simply because it is God's will, is only an animal resistance which beasts show to better advantage than mankind. Such a resistance is too narrow in its scope and gross in its results. The true spirit of resistance is that which compels man to rise superior to his surroundings, to conquer victory out of defeat, to combat hostile nature as well as human adversaries, and to throw up and maintain perpetual fortifications against the insidious attrition of natural and physical decay. It is a resistance which can be as unyielding as bands of steel and as pliable as a silken zone. It was transported across the ocean in the pilgrim ship, and found a kindly refuge on New England soil. It tugged and toiled and sweat and froze until the village had succeeded the wigwam, the broad highway the Indian trail, fair cities and towns decked these hills and vales, and sails spread themselves as gallantly to the new-world winds as to the old. The church and the school-house softened the rough edges, but took out none of its God-given temper, which was always as tried and true as the Damascus blade in its silken sheath. It sounded the fife and drum of '75, and faltered not when a victor held the blood-stained crest on Bunker Hill. It joyfully went back to the plundered home and wasted farm when British grenadier and Hessian dragoon had sailed away with muffled drums and drooping plumes. It founded an empire of which we all, to-day, can thank God we are constituent parts, — not merely an empire of wealth and numerical strength, but an empire of thought, of liberty, of education, with a glorious past behind it, and the positive promise of a still more glorious future.

It was this God-sent and Heaven-directed attribute of resistance, fed by the rough winds of our rugged coast, nourished by the breath of our pines, which stirred this young physician's pulse and nerved his heart to divide his time between the couches of his patients and the public business. For as early as 1774 we find he was Secretary of the Bristol County Convention, called then to take measures concerning the public safety, and to provide for the impending struggle; and in the autumn of the same year the town of Taunton, already appreciating his wisdom and sagacity, sent him, as you have stated, to the General Court as the colleague of Robert Treat Paine, of holy memory, where, no doubt, in those days just prior to the sacrifices of Lexington and Bunker Hill, his voice was often heard urging others to follow the course that he soon after pursued; for, in 1777, as Lieutenant-Colonel of the Sixteenth Massachusetts Regiment, known as the Boston Regiment, and commanded by Colonel Henry Jackson, he too accepted the grim chances of war. The Sixteenth soon found active service in the Jerseys. It was in the thickest of the fray at the terrible battle of Monmouth; and later at our nearer battle at Quaker Hill, Rhode Island, where it led the forlorn-hope in the charge against the Hessian cavalry, which had been such a scourge upon the people. His bravery and judgment soon attracted the attention of the Commander-in-Chief; and, in 1781, we find he was transferred from the Sixteenth Regiment to the staff of Washington, where of five he was the second in point of rank. Of the pregnant years that followed to the close of the war, time will not allow me to speak ; suffice it to say that the joys and successes, the sorrows and disappointments of his illustrious commander were all alike his. With him he witnessed the closing scenes of the war, the surrender of Cornwallis, and, at that time, so great was the attachment of Washington to him, that he retired with him, after the close of hostilities, to Mount Vernon, where he passed a number of months as a member of the great commander's family, and one of his most intimate friends.

In 1784 General Cobb returned to Massachusetts, intending then to begin his labors where he had left off prior to taking up arms. He proposed to renew the practice of medicine in the town of Taunton. But the public service needed him then more than the sick couches of his patients, and he was at once commissioned a Judge of the Court of Common Pleas, by the Governor of Massachusetts, and took his seat upon the bench. At the same time, or shortly after, he was made Major-General of the Fifth Division of Massachusetts Militia. It was in 1786 that the discontents which were left as a legacy from the Revolution, took that form which has come down to us in history as the Shays' Rebellion, and in Bristol County, as elsewhere, the courts were the special objects of attack. An armed mob, gathered from all portions of the county, led by one Colonel Valentine, who had seen service in the Revolution, marched upon the town of Taunton, one day when the court was in session. The military was called out, and the Judge and Major-General took command. To the demands of the rioters that the court should adjourn and the papers be given up, he made that memorable reply, sir, which you have quoted, " I will hold this court if I hold it in blood; I will sit as a judge or I will die as a general." Convinced that there was stuff before them too determined to be trifled with, the mob slunk away. They failed to raise their courage to the sticking-point until October of the same year, when again, armed and unarmed, a howling, tumultuous, disorderly band, they took their way to Taunton, where the court was in session, and reiterated the demands that they had made before. They desired that the court should be dissolved; they wanted the papers; they wished to put an end to the farce which was called justice. The Major-General (Judge Cobb) ordered a field-piece — which is now in a good state of preservation and the gift of a colored Revolutionary soldier to the town of Taunton — to be placed in position in front of the court-house. He had it loaded with canister shot to the very muzzle, and placed a cannoneer by its side with a lighted match. To the demand of the mob that the court should be dissolved, and that they should have the papers, he replied, " If you want these papers you must come and take them, but I will fire on the first man that crosses the line." This, again, was sufficient; the mob had had enough of General Cobb; Colonel Valentine withdrew his men, and armed resistance to judicial authority was heard of no more in Bristol County. Perhaps if there had been a soldier-judge on the bench in some other counties of the State at that time, a more honorable story could be told of them in those trying times.

In 1789 General Cobb was sent again to the State House in Boston. Recognizing his accomplishments, his associates in the Legislature chose him Speaker, and for four years he exercised the responsible duties of that office to the complete satisfaction of his associates and the State. In 1793 he was elected a representative from Massachusetts to the Third Congress. He remained in Congress two years, and in 1795 returned to Massachusetts. He was not allowed to rest nor waste his time in what the people considered in those days a profession unworthy of him. He was at once appointed Chief Justice of the Court of Common Pleas of the District of Maine, which was then a part of the Commonwealth of Massachusetts. He remained there till 1801, when he was sent to the Massachusetts Senate to represent what was known as the Eastern District of Maine. His residence, I think, was in the town of Goldsborough. He was at once chosen President of the body, and for four years he presided over its destinies. Then he retired till the year 1808, when he was a member of the Executive Council; in 1809 he was the Lieutenant-Governor of the Commonwealth; in 1812, when the cloud of war again darkened the country, he was made Major-General of the Tenth Military Division, with headquarters on the coast of Maine; in 1813 he was one of the Committee of Safety of those days. In 1820 General Cobb left Maine, and returned to his old home in Taunton, where he passed the remaining years of his life. Dying in 1830 in this city, his remains were conveyed to Taunton, and were there interred.

From one who remembers him well, I learn that he

was of large stature, full, florid face, and commanding presence. When engaged in his official duties as a jurist, he wore the cocked hat of the revolutionary period, breeches with band and buckles, white top-boots, and marched into the court-room with the air of a general about to review his division on dress parade. Perfectly in keeping with his manner, his court was managed with military precision, and at the sharp word of command from the bench there was immediate obedience on the part of bar and officials. Straightforward himself, he despised all shams; and it is characteristic of the man that he once said to a lawyer whose actions he thought were open to suspicion, " Sir, a dishonest lawyer is worse than the devil, for he violates personal confidence and a sacred trust!" Courteous in manner, stately and dignified, possessed of a fund of anecdote of the court, the camp, and the legislature, he was a most genial companion, and one whom all who knew him, and their names certainly were legion, were proud to honor. Besides the honors which fell to him in course from his own Alma Mater, he was made an honorary Master of Arts by Brown University; he had the same degree from the College of New Jersey, he was a member of the Massachusetts Medical Society, of the American Society of Arts and Sciences, and Vice-President of the Society of the Cincinnati.

It is a pleasant duty, Mr. President, to welcome to these walls the portrait of one whose active years were so occupied with the public business that one fairly starts with wonder when he reflects how varied were his accomplishments, how trying the situations in which he was called upon to act, and how honorably and worthily he wrought out his life-work. And he was blessed in this, that his life was spared to see the fruition of the most ardent hopes of his youth. He lived to see the thirteen discordant Colonies pass through the crucible of the Revolution and emerge as the nucleus of a republic fairer and brighter than the wildest dream of any colonial seer. He lived to see the frontier pushed further and further towards the setting sun, and new Commonwealths arise from the desolation of the wilderness, clad in the full apparel of civilization, until the thirteen had been swelled to twenty-seven, and the four million people of 1790 had become the fourteen million of 1830. He lived to see the white sails of commerce thicken in every harbor; he lived to hear the clatter of machinery and the clank of the anvil drown the footsteps of the disappearing savage; he lived to welcome the first ripple of that great flood-tide of immigration from the old world, and forecast the possibilities of the pregnant future. He died full of years and full of labors; and the Commonwealth honors him, but honors itself more this day that it places his picture on these walls among the representative men of historic epochs.

But, Mr. President, in contemplating these features, which we hope future generations will also honor and reverence, let us not forget that the stars of the historic firmament which we are permitted to see and study are but few in number in comparison with the vast multitude who have been buried in the haze of oblivion, yet to whom, too, we owe a boundless debt of honor and of gratitude. Perhaps if these silent lips could speak, they would say to us, " We accept this honor, not merely for ourselves, but for the innumerable multitude, the silent

and forgotten dead on the field of battle, whose record is
locked up in the echoless chambers of oblivion." It is
ever true that the nobler impulses of the mind, — love
of liberty, resistance to oppression, devotion to country, —
rising superior to mere fear of bodily harm, has turned
the tenderest into soldiers, with muscles of iron and
hearts of granite, and rallied into a resistless wave a
martial array, which neither biting frosts, nor tropic
suns, nor malarious death-damps, nor all of the agonies
of shot or shell could baffle, till victory or death was
the glorious culmination. Heroes have begotten heroes
since the earth was young, and at the roll-call of the his-
torian the ranks of the heroic dead start forth in bris-
tling columns, with stone axe and club, with bronze
arrow and spear, with blade of steel and linked cuirass,
with homespun coat and clumsy gun, with crooked
scimitar and poisoned dart, with broadsword and bayonet,
or with no weapon save that undaunted breast, which no
torture of the trembling flesh could terrify until victory
or death was the glorious culmination. All races, all
colors, all creeds, are there in that grim array, broad
and well-defined at first, as it winds through the nearer
centuries, but shadowy and indistinct as it leads back
through those distant years which brought forth their
living and buried their dead before the pen arose, like
another star in the east, to light the course of the world.
So it will be unto the end of time. The resistant spirit,
born with the first hero, died not when his mortal
body was laid away. It lives on, eternal and unchange-
able. The lapse of years affects not its powers nor dims
its brightness. Like the cloudy pillar by day and the
crimson glow by night, it lights up the course of historic

triumphs, no matter to what epoch the scrutinizing glass of the student of history is turned. The breasts which swelled at Marathon a living wall against myriad Persian spears, throbbed with new life at Lexington ; the heroes of Thermopylæ renewed their vows at Concord Bridge ; the ten thousand of Attic story again dragged their weary march from Lookout to the sea ; the bleeding ranks of Waterloo, mangled by shot and torn by shell, sprinkled Wagner's thirsty sands with gore, and clove through the smoke and flame of hell to Petersburg's death-girdled breach. No narrow grave can contain the heroic spirit. Borne to the earth, it drinks in new strength from the great mother. Whenever the sword of freedom waves, the might of ages nerves the arm that wields it ; and whenever a pæan of victory arises, in honor of a glorious success deserved as well as won, myriads of voices from myriads of graves join in the grateful song. We only read the future by the past, and, by the lessons we have learned, we know that, if on the morrow the long roll should sound and the alarm-bell clang, it would not be necessary for us to speed away o'er troubled seas to seek the great Achilles, whom we knew, but we should find him full armored, with weapons bright, in the heart of every liberty-loving citizen.

Hon. WILLIAM H. HAILE, Senator from Hampden, said : —

General David Cobb was, indeed, a gentleman of the old school. He was a man who always performed his duty in whatever sphere of action he was called to take a part. He was one of that class of men who builded better than they knew, — men whose motives were so pure, whose actions were so just, as to command the respect and confidence of all with whom they were brought in contact. It was owing to such men that this republic was able to free itself from the power of Great Britain, and to begin that wonderful career of progress and growth which has never yet been equalled in the annals of history. And although General Cobb lived to see that country for which he perilled his life increase much in population and resources, yet neither he nor his compeers could have believed that this land would attain its present proud position among the nations of the earth, and that the possibilities lying before it would be so vast and so glorious. The various offices, both civil and military, which General Cobb held during his life, show the esteem and confidence in which he was held by his fellow-citizens. As has been said, during the War of the Revolution he was one of the aides of General Washington, and, better still, he was Washington's friend. In these days of partisan strife and personal ambitions, how the pure and noble character of Washington stands out in contrast; and to have been his personal, trusted friend, that were indeed an honor greatly to be prized. The quelling of the mob by General Cobb in Taunton in 1786 brings to our minds the fact that at that time, in the western part of this Commonwealth, in the city which I have the honor to represent in this Senate to-day, what was known as the Shays' Rebellion, of which this Taunton mob was but a part, received its overthrow. The causes which led to this rebellion were various. The War of the Revolution had just been brought to a close; trade was stagnant; land was almost valueless; poverty, ruin, starvation stared many of the people in the face. The National Constitution had not then become the law of the land, and there was at least a minority who did not believe in the workings of our State Constitution. What wonder, then, that men in their desperation, when they saw their homes taken from them on executions in favor of their creditors, and their families turned out of doors, should be filled with discontent, and led to rise in rebellion? Suppose these same causes should occur to-day, would not there be equal danger of turmoil and bloodshed? But in this case, when the line was sharply drawn between law and order on the one side and confusion and perhaps anarchy on the other, then the self-sacrificing spirit which animated the heroes of the Revolution pervaded the people at this critical period, and the attack on the National Arsenal at Springfield ended in the repulse of the rebels, and the downfall of the rebellion. All honor, then, to General Lincoln and General Shepard, brother officers of General Cobb in the War of the Revolution, for the promptness and the good judgment that they displayed in subduing the last rebellion in this Commonwealth.

That this portrait should adorn the walls of this Senate Chamber seems very fitting, because, as has been said, General Cobb was one of the illustrious Presidents of this Senate. He presided over it, as we are told, fourscore years ago, with unrivalled grace. And in looking upon the face on that canvas, we can but confess that the Senate, in electing him its presiding officer, did confer great honor upon itself. For what he was and for what he did, his likeness and his memory should be perpetuated, not only within these walls, but throughout this Commonwealth. He was a wise and skilful physician, a daring soldier, one born to command, an upright and just magistrate, a patriot and a statesman, a man who perilled his life and gave his all in the service of his country in the hour of its greatest need. Surely a man possessed of these attributes is entitled to the grateful remembrance of the people. Representing this State, in what has sometimes been called the celebrated Third Congress, he became associated with such men as Madison, Ames, and others of like repute, — men, by whose good judgment, great intellect, and unerring sagacity, the progress and the growth of the new republic seemed to be assured. It is not strange that the name of General Cobb should now be unfamiliar to many. His death occurred fifty years ago, and it is but the truth to say that many of his contemporaries, men who won great distinction and who did much in the public and private walks of life, are scarcely remembered to-day. We do well to study the lives of these men.

Mr. President, as we accept this portrait and as we heartily thank the generous donor for his most suitable gift, may we also express the hope that hereafter, when members of future Senates and the people come here and look upon the portrait of General David Cobb, they may be led to study his character, and be inspired to emulate his virtues.

Hon. CHESTER C. CORBIN, Senator from Worcester, said : —

After the most appropriate resolutions, and the very eloquent remarks of those who have preceded me, it not only is unnecessary, but would be in the poorest of taste for me to undertake to add aught to what has been already said in praise of the man whom we this day honor. Yet, there is one thought in connection with this occasion which possibly I may be pardoned for trespassing upon your time if I present. In olden time great stress was laid upon good blood, and the line of family descent was accounted of the most value in determining individual worth. I have no desire to disparage this idea, yet I am constrained to say that in these later times good deeds, noble actions that spring from right motives, count for more than do the accidents of birth and blood. The young men of to-day need to be impressed with the thought that actual worth is the real test of manhood, and whatever tends to bring this thought to the mind, in its relationship to the men of the past, is worthy of our consideration.

Of many a man it may be truthfully said that " he being dead, yet speaketh." It is not simply the canvas upon which we gaze, however radiant it may be with life, but rather the record of that life. It is an *open volume* upon which we look, and on its pages we read, in letters of living light, the record of a worthy and well-spent life. It is a *lesson* presented for our study. This is a thoroughly busy world, and its inhabitants, as a class, do not have time for careful study. The bronze or marble statue of hero, poet, or painter; the life-speaking canvas is, of itself, a condensed history, an epitome of many printed volumes, so plainly written that even he who runs may read. The face upon which we gaze, even though it has not life, yet speaks. The form which thus is represented, though it cannot move, yet walks forth amongst men, not in form and figure, but in thought and character. Many a man's life represents a struggle for some great principle, a protest against some

4

great wrong, and shall the struggle end with the life? Shall the protest die with the man? No! Like as the face and form of the commander stimulates the soldier in the hour of strife, so shall this face and form, as it looks down upon us and our successors, call us and them to stronger work and nobler purpose. In Doric Hall below, we look upon the marble form of John A. Andrew, and from the sight we go forth with a new stimulus and an enlarged patriotism. We look at the chiselled statue of Webster, as it stands in all its massive strength, and we catch *his* voice as in clarion notes it breaks upon the ear, and we go forth to duty with a keener appreciation of manhood's worth.

I have somewhere read the story of a painting that hung upon the walls of an old castle. It was the likeness of one who, in his lifetime, was a warrior and a statesman. Those who came after him failed to possess the virtue and manhood of himself. The nation was drifting to decay. One day, when the land seemed lost to all honor and noble deed, this hero stepped from the canvas, endowed anew with life, that he might once again inspire the people with his own valor and lead them anew to victory! We cannot expect that out from this canvas shall come forth to new life this man who has already done his share in life; but we may expect, as we look upon his face, a new inspiration to duty, and a louder call to life's work.

Hon. NATHANIEL A. HORTON, Senator from Essex, said:—

Mr. President, — The exercises of this hour are commemorative of a representative character of the Revolutionary period, and they are also the appropriate accompaniment of an act by which a respected descendant of an honored ancestor pays an appropriate tribute to a memory worthy of being cherished, and at the same time places within the view of those who visit or from year to year gather within this Chamber, one more of those silent but expressive memorials which connect the past with the present, and which tend to the development of an ideal standard both of public and private life which is not otherwise than beneficial to society and promotive of the best interest of the State.

The portraits which hang within this Legislative Chamber, representing the men who have occupied high positions of honor and trust within this Commonwealth, — John Winthrop, John Endicott, John Leverett, Simon Bradstreet, and the rest, — have a significance not measured altogether by their official character nor by the simple record of their lives. They are types of the men who made and have given character to this Commonwealth. The youth who enters and looks around this Chamber, casting his eyes musingly upon these portraits sees in them an ideal standard of patriotism and rectitude in public life which of itself may be a potent influence in shaping his own character, his own destiny, and his own influence in the walks of men.

The character which to-day takes its place among the memorials of this hall, is not widely known. In the history of human affairs, even men of more than ordinary mark and distinction in their day drop out from public sight, and in a few generations are forgotten. The names in history which stand forth and come down through the centuries to be mentioned with the familiarity of household words, are comparatively few. There is no claim that this man was one of these. He was not a type of what we call the famous men in history, but rather a conspicuous illustration of the public capacity to produce the men to fill stations of responsibility and trust in times of emergency; and of that stern integrity, unselfish patriotism, and capacity to grasp the essential principles of a well organized society, which were so conspicuous a trait among those plain men whose judgment and moral support were as essential an element in the formation of this Republic, as the leadership of those master minds which have become renowned in the annals of American statesmanship.

If I should feel inclined to welcome this memorial upon one ground more than another, it would be upon the presumption that it typifies these particular qualities in our early American life. It was in the prevalence of these qualities that our system of government was founded and placed upon a firm and broad basis of enduring principles. Upon the extent to which these qualities are preserved will depend the future welfare of our institutions.

I am not unwilling, Mr. President, to be classed among those men of conservative tendencies who hold in veneration the marvellous wisdom, foresight, and mental grasp which laid down and incorporated into law the rules and safeguards upon which a popular government must rely for its successful administration. And I should always be slow to counsel changes in our methods of administering justice, or in the fundamental law of our Commonwealth, if they seemed to be of a nature likely to prove eventually destructive of those wise safeguards which the founders of our system so carefully and thoughtfully considered, and the wisdom of which has been proved by the experience of a century.

This man whom we here commemorate, I infer from a somewhat hasty examination of his career, was one who had his share of the faults common to men. A biographer has said he was " hasty in temper." It is easy to imagine, both from this record, and from certain acts of determination recorded in his official life, that he possessed qualities that would not, of themselves, have been likely to secure for him that advancement to representative positions which marked his life. His elevation to one public trust after another was evidently due largely to an honesty of purpose, earnestness of conviction, and determination to stand by every principle which he deemed vital to the welfare and preservation of a popular government ; and, viewing his selection for public trusts in this light, it was not more honorable to his character than to the discriminating judgment of the constituencies who selected him to represent their interests. His life, viewed in this aspect, is valuable as a tribute to American character, and as an evidence of the faith which may safely be reposed in the controlling mass of intelligent men. The majority of people do not dislike a marked individuality of character in any man. They will elevate men of earnest and sincere convictions, and, as a rule, will rely upon the judgment of such in the performance of public trusts. The senator or the representative who stands by an honest and intelligent conviction, even though it seems to be at variance with an apparent popular sentiment of a passing hour, will, as a rule, better and more acceptably represent the enduring sentiment of the people, than the one whose chief solicitude is to arrive at an estimate of what will best please a majority of his constituents in the transitory judgment of a passing hour.

The man who best subserves the highest purpose in life is he whose acts are inspired by a sense of personal responsibility of which he is not conscious, just as the men who seem to have fulfilled the greatest mission in life are those who appear to have been the least conscious that they had a mission. As a rule, in the conduct and consideration of public affairs, the man who is inspired by high principles and sincere convictions, and who is animated by an honest purpose to engraft them upon a community, in his daily walk as a citizen and in the exercise of his influence at the ballot-box, is the man whose inspiration is that of an instinctive and unstudied sense of personal responsibility for the influence he may exert. To such men, life is regarded as a trust, and none the less so regarded because they do not stop to reason out the problem of living, nor carefully calculate their destiny in the great future that is beyond.

Mr. President, it is of no consequence to the world at large, nor even to those who are gathered here, but to me the thought is full of interesting suggestiveness, that this man passed out of life the day following that on which I came into life. He and I dwelt one day together in the land of the living. And thus the world goes on. One man goes out and another comes in. The change is constant, and the law never fails. A man drops out, and, even where he has filled positions of distinction, he is soon forgotten, and, if his name comes accidentally to the surface, men mouse among musty records to find trace of who and what he was. It is a wonderful thought that at intervals of comparatively few years this entire earth is repeopled. " One generation passeth away, and another generation cometh." And yet we come into life singly, and at intervals apart, and we drop out of life in the same way. The young jostle along for a period with the old, and the old with the young. Each exerts its influence upon the other, and no man has a right to say or to think that his influence counts for nothing in the world's economy. It is a matter of little consequence in human affairs whether we are honored with the distinctions which men bestow. It is of great consequence that we realize the responsibility of the trust which is imposed in whatever station and calling in life we occupy.

It is largely to this unstudied sense of responsibility, in the conduct of public affairs more particularly, that we are indebted for the wise provisions of government which we enjoy to-day. To me this portrait, which is hereafter to grace these walls, will have its chief and most valuable significance, not in the fact that it recalls a man who was an aide to Washington, valuable and patriotic as that memory may be ; nor in the fact that he occupied the chair of the President of the Senate, interesting as that no doubt is to us all ; but in the fact that he was a type of that manhood which is ever alive to a sense of its public duties, and of that individuality of character which has proved so valuable a trait in the stock from which we sprung, and which has made this State and this country all that they now are.

Hon. GEORGE A. BRUCE, Senator from Middlesex, spoke as
follows: —

Mr. President, — I join most heartily in what has
already been said, expressive of the thanks which are
due from the Senate and the Commonwealth to the generous donor of this splendid canvas. It is an acquisition
of which we may well be proud, judged not only as a
work of art, but as a lifelike presentment of the features
of one of Massachusetts' illustrious public characters. Indeed, I think we might go further and say that individ-
ually at least our thanks are due for the opportunity of
listening to the exercises thus far completed of this most
pleasant occasion. There has been withdrawn from
before us, as it were. the veil which separates us from
the past. We have been permitted to look again upon
the features of a buried generation, and to hear portrayed the strong and manly traits of character which
well entitles the portrait of David Cobb to a place side
by side with those of the other Massachusetts men that
now grace and adorn these walls.

I remember to have heard it said of Thoreau, the
poet naturalist, that, if by some charm he could have
been put to sleep for a century and then could wake in
any season of the year, he could without the aid of human agency tell the very day of the month, so familiar
to his eye were all the secrets of nature about him, —
the mysteries, to most of us, of earth and air, of plant,
of tree, of cloud and sky.

It seems to me that, without the aid of name or date,
from the noble face that looks out to us from yonder

canvas, from the portraiture of character so finely and skilfully drawn by the accomplished presiding officer of this body, and by the cultured Senator from Bristol, we should each of us have been led to suspect that we were looking upon the features of one who belonged to what has been aptly termed the heroic age in Massachusetts; there was in and of him so much of that tough mental fibre, so much of that resolute and unconquerable will, so much of those other high mental and moral qualities which every one familiar with history recognizes as belonging to the men who struck the chains of servitude from this people and clothed them with freedom regulated by law.

The man who uttered the noble sentiment at Taunton Court House, twice repeated this afternoon, might well have given expression to the sentiment which is involuntarily suggested at the mention of the name of Henry, or that other of equal renown which is inseparably connected with the name of the elder Adams.

It was said of Mirabeau that a word from him marked an epoch in the French Revolution; of James Otis, that by his electric eloquence he brought a continent to its feet; of John Adams, that he lifted the American Colonies up to independence. What wonderful powers of condensed expression we admire in such men. Life with them seemed too short and events too pressing to allow the waste of moments even in useless speech. A sentence in passionate and burning words, voicing the aspirations and ardent hopes of a people, has more than once in history cut the Gordian knot and changed the destiny of nations.

But after all it is not so much the words, as Emerson puts it, as the man behind the words. It was not so much the short and pithy sentence of General Cobb at Taunton Green as the man behind it that awed and quelled the crowd.

How marked are the times in which he lived and acted, and how contrasted with those in which he now comes in miniature to again take up his abode among us. We are now living as it were in a great civic calm, — thanks to him and such as he, — the bounds of freedom widely and firmly set, personal liberty secure and safe under a wise and beneficent system of laws.

As one passes the Berkshire Hills and travels westward in the summer time day after day through level fields of waving grain and corn, ten times larger than the whole acreage of Massachusetts, he is apt to feel that here at home we are somewhat isolated and circumscribed within altogether too narrow limits. But we feel and know that the greatness of States cannot be measured by material things. Here as elsewhere the world of thought and action that knows no bounds is open to us, and all who wish may enter it. Massachusetts has entered it, and here it is that by her children she has won her great and imperishable renown. Life with us is broader and richer for their achievements. We live not alone in the present, but that which has gone before and that which we devoutly hope will come hereafter enter into and form in part the enjoyments of the passing hour.

No State has been more fortunate than Massachusetts in the character of her public men in each epoch of her history ; and no State cherishes their names with more of pride and satisfaction.   It was while thinking of these and of the generations of noble men and women too, who have lived and passed away with them, that Whittier gave expression to the sentiment with which we should all here be in sympathy and accord : —

> " Then ask not why to these rough hills
>   I cling, as clings the tufted moss,
>   To bear the winter's lingering chills,
>   The mocking spring's perpetual loss ;
>   I dream of lands where summer smiles,
>   Where soft winds blow from spicy isles ;
>   But scarce would Ceylon's breath of flowers be sweet,
>   Could I not feel thy soil, New England, at my feet."

Hon. PELEG McFARLIN, Senator from Plymouth, said : —

Though I may not hope to command the stately utterance best suited to this hour, still I cannot permit the occasion to pass without expressing something of the sense of obligation I feel, in common with my associates, towards the donor of this most worthy and appropriate gift. It is certainly most appropriate that one whose name is indissolubly associated with the early struggles of the Republic, and who, in later days, won distinction in these halls as a patriot and a statesman, should take his place here, in full and equal companionship with these other worthies whose faces adorn this Senate Chamber through the subtle reproduction of art.   It is strikingly appropriate that a lineal descendant of him whose virtues we this day commemorate, who has himself done the State some service, who has wisely presided over the destinies of this New England metropolis, who, by his

conspicuous talents, has signally illustrated the principle
of hereditary transmission, should from his own munifi-
cence present this portrait to his mother State. From a
full heart I thank him for the costly offering he this day
submits to our keeping. And, Mr. President, I cannot
say too much in praise of this painting. As I look on
that heroic face, which wears its dignity so well, it seems
to kindle with the pulse of life, and with the illumination
of thought. The lips seem to stir again with the old-time
eloquence, inspiring the heart with reverence for the
past, and with exultant hope for the future. Let Massachusetts guard well the memory of this Revolutionary
sire. Let the sculptor vie with the painter in perpetu-
ating his mortal charms, till the lines of Whittier,
written in eulogy of Sumner, shall become equally
applicable to General Cobb: —

> " The marble image of her son
> Her loving hands shall yearly crown ;
> And, from her pictured pantheon,
> His grand, majestic face look down."

The resolution was unanimously adopted by a rising vote.

www.ingramcontent.com/pod-product-compliance
Lightning Source LLC
Chambersburg PA
CBHW032142080426
42733CB00008B/1165